Plants for shade

Cover:

The shade-loving *Actaea rubra* is known as baneberry because of its poisonous berries (photograph by Michael Warren)

Overleaf: snowdrops growing in the shade of a tree; these are *Galanthus nivalis* 'Sam Arnott', with large scented flowers

Plants for shade

A Wisley handbook

Fay Sharman

Cassell

The Royal Horticultural Society

Cassell Educational Limited
Artillery House, Artillery Row
London SW1P 1RT
for the Royal Horticultural Society

First published 1988
Reprinted 1989

British Library Cataloguing in Publication Data

Sharman, Fay
Plants for shade.——(A Wisley handbook).
1. Shade-tolerant plants——Great Britain
I. Title II. Royal Horticultural Society
635.9′54 SB434.7

ISBN 0–304–31102–2

Photographs by Michael Warren and the Harry Smith Collection
Design by Lesley Stewart
Phototypesetting by Chapterhouse, The Cloisters, Formby
Printed in Hong Kong by Wing King Tong Co. Ltd.

Contents

Introduction

Shade is an integral part of the natural landscape, where trees, shrubs, perennials, bulbs and grasses coexist at different levels in a harmonious whole. The most effective garden is based on the same principle, of planting in layers, and contains a mixture of sun- and shade-loving plants. A totally shadeless garden would be a dull and artificial place, lacking the subtle effects, the contrasts between light and dark and the sense of tranquillity which shade can provide.

There are many plants which actually prefer shade, including not only numerous shrubs, but herbaceous perennials, bulbs, ferns and annuals. Although often less flamboyant than sun-lovers, they compensate in various ways – with delicately coloured flowers, a long season of bloom, attractive foliage or fruits, a graceful habit. In addition to the active shade-lovers, some versatile plants succeed in sun or shade, even if they may be less floriferous in the latter. The Mexican orange blossom, *Choisya ternata*, for example, is content with a sunless corner or against a south-facing wall. However, there is no point trying resolutely sun-loving plants in shade: they will soon show their dislike of such a position by becoming pale and drawn, with lanky thin stems, large floppy leaves and few, if any, flowers.

Shade can be a great asset in the garden, offering the opportunity to grow a host of delightful plants. However, there are several degrees of shade and, the denser it is, the more restricted the choice of plants. While many woodland plants enjoy the dappled shade of trees and others appreciate partial shade, where they are protected from the hottest sun, very few can survive in deep permanent shade. Similarly, certain plants may grow well in the open shade of a wall or building, but be unable to tolerate the heavy direct shade beneath a tree, which is made worse by drip from the leaves and competition from the roots. This is where shade can be a challenge to the gardener, not a blessing, and it is a common problem in the typical small garden of today.

Opposite: *Oxalis acetosella* 'Rosea', a pink-flowered wood sorrel, thrives in dappled shade

Shade in the garden

ASSESSING THE SITUATION

It is rarely possible to reduce the amount of shade in a garden, where this is caused by existing features such as walls, buildings or tall overhanging trees. In a small town or suburban garden, some parts inevitably receive little or no sunshine.

If you are buying a house, it is important to check the orientation of its garden. Remember that the extent of shade varies considerably according to the time of year and that, as the day progresses from sunrise to sunset, there is a continual movement of shadows. It is always worth observing a new garden through the seasons before deciding what can be grown where.

The selection and positioning of plants requires forward planning. A frequent mistake is to underestimate the rate of growth of a tree or shrub and to find that, within a few years, its shadow has encroached on a previously sunny bed. Regional differences in climate should also be taken into account. The south and east of Britain tend to be hotter and drier than the rest of the country: here plants may rely on shade to supply the cool moist conditions they need, whereas in the colder or wetter north and west they can thrive in full sun.

A shady garden can be just as rewarding as a sunny one, if you make the most of each area by using suitable plants – climbers to enhance a north-facing wall, frost-tender shrubs taking advantage of the shelter of an enclosed space, woodlanders in the filtered light beneath trees. A damp place in the shade could be converted into a bog garden and, as a last resort, there are some cosmetic solutions for those really awkward dark spots, where almost nothing will grow.

TYPES OF SHADE

It is extremely hard to define degrees of shade, especially since these are linked to other factors like soil conditions and the nature of the site. However, it is useful to distinguish initially three broad categories, which will have a bearing on the choice of plants:

1 *Permanent shade*

a) A dark corner or similar enclosed spot which is always in shade, because the sun is excluded by nearby obstacles, such as a building, wall or fence, an evergreen hedge or tree.

The beautiful 'Maigold' is one of several roses which can be grown on a north-facing wall

b) A north-facing border or wall which experiences constant shade but is open to the sky.

2 *Partial shade*

An area which is in shadow for part of the day as the sun moves across the sky.

3 *Dappled shade*

An area beneath a high thin canopy of deciduous trees, whose leaves and branches filter the sunlight.

SHADE FROM TREES

As major sources of shade, trees present special problems. One of the most serious is that their roots rob the surrounding soil of the moisture and food needed by other plants. Beech and birch are notoriously greedy, although the deeper-rooting oak is more accommodating. Hedges, particularly privet with its invasive roots, can make planting equally difficult. In all these cases, thorough preparation of the soil is vital if plants are to succeed.

Trees cast shade to varying degrees. There is the perpetual deep shade of a dense evergreen tree, such as holly, and the summertime shade of a deciduous tree, which may be heavy or light according to the size, shape and quantity of leaves. Small leaves and open branches produce the pleasant dappled shade favoured by many plants. On the other hand, large leaves or dense overlapping foliage, of horse chestnut or beech for example, effectively block out the light and also allow very little rain to penetrate. Few plants will grow in the heavy shade beneath them.

An additional factor is the height and form of the tree. A tall upright tree with a straight trunk will admit more light, as well as rain, than a spreading tree with low branches, to the greater benefit of plants underneath. Light can be improved to a certain extent by removing some of the lower branches of a tree and thinning out the crown, but care must be taken not to spoil the overall appearance. The distance between trees, too, will obviously influence the amount of light reaching the ground.

With deciduous trees, the timing of leaf development is yet another consideration. A horse chestnut will normally have completed its canopy of foliage by mid-May, so that very little apart from spring-flowering bulbs can be planted below it, whereas a walnut will not be in full leaf until July, enabling a wider variety of plants to be grown. Similarly, some trees keep their foliage later in the season than others, which affects the use of the ground beneath. When the leaves fall each autumn, they supply valuable organic material to the soil, from which lesser plants can profit, although there is an attendant risk of smothering if the leaves are large and heavy like those of the sycamore. Drip from trees can also cause damage.

SOIL

Closely linked with the basic types of shade are the soil conditions, which may range from dry to moist and acid to alkaline. These too will determine the choice of plants.

Probably the easiest shady place to plant is the edge of a pond or bank of a stream, where there is a plentiful supply of water. Many plants revel in such a situation, among them primulas and hostas. In fact, most shade-lovers prefer to be moist and cool. The problem areas are those of dry shade and unfortunately they tend to be in the majority – beside walls or high buildings and under overhanging eaves, where little rain reaches the soil, and beneath trees or near hedges, whose roots compete for any rainfall which does penetrate.

The goat's beard, *Aruncus dioicus*, is a spectacular plant for dappled shade, particularly in moist soil

Dry soils in shade need thorough preparation before planting, incorporating as much bulky organic material as possible to retain moisture. Home-made compost, leafmould or peat are suitable and should be dug into the top layer of soil. This preliminary digging and improvement of the soil is particularly important on new sites, where the earth has often become dry and compacted by machinery and may be full of builder's rubble.

Aquilegia long-spurred hybrids compose a pleasant picture in shade

A mulch of similar material, after planting, will also help to conserve moisture in the soil. It should be spread in a layer about 2 in. (5 cm) thick, tucking it between the plants, and is best applied annually in late February or early March.

Cultivation of the soil is not always possible, in rooty ground under a tree, for instance, or on a steep bank. Here the answer could be to clear the area with a contact non-persistent weedkiller (for instance, paraquat and diquat) and then plant vigorous ground-covering plants, such as periwinkle, *Vinca major*, or the rose of Sharon, *Hypericum calycinum*.

The chemical composition of the soil also plays a part in the selection of plants. The degree of acidity is expressed by the pH scale: a neutral soil has a pH of 7, below 7 is acid and above alkaline. Soil pH can be measured with a simple soil-testing kit. The majority of plants enjoy a neutral to slightly acid soil, although many are tolerant of a wide range of conditions. It is only the extremes which cause difficulty. Fortunately, however, some of the most beautiful shade-lovers require and thrive on acid soil, notably rhododendrons and camellias. At the other end of the scale, plants like clematis, osmanthus and the invaluable *Choisya ternata* succeed in shade on alkaline soil, even in a shallow dry soil over chalk.

Choosing plants for shade

The following suggestions for plants to grow in various types of shade are by no means exhaustive, but may be taken as representative. In many cases, the categories overlap and it is often worth experimenting with plants in different situations.

The plants are divided into two groups – shrubs first and then other plants, including herbaceous perennials, bulbs, ferns and grasses – and are listed under their botanical names in alphabetical order. It is not possible to give precise dimensions for plants, as they will vary to some extent according to conditions, and the measurements are intended merely as a guide.

PERMANENT DEEP SHADE

Dark corners, narrow passages between houses, basements and other enclosed spaces, where the sun never penetrates, are a common problem. This all-the-year-round shade can be suffocating to plants, particularly if, as often happens, the soil is dry and lifeless or dank and mossy. The advice given on thorough soil preparation is all the more applicable in such conditions and the addition of moisture-retentive material is vital.

An area like this is so definite that it basically dictates the range of plants which can be grown there. However, various devices can help to improve appearances. Painting the walls a paler colour or white brings light to a dark corner and provides a good background for foliage and flowers, showing off both shapes and colours. Light-coloured paving and white trellis could also be introduced. Similarly, plants with variegated or yellow-flushed leaves will brighten the effect, although in some cases the markings may fade in the restricted light. Silver foliage plants, unfortunately, rarely succeed in shade.

Building a raised bed is another idea if one wants to get the most out of a confined area. It adds a new dimension of interest, breaking up any flatness and detracting from the apparent height of surrounding walls. It has practical advantages too, where the existing soil is worn out or poorly drained, since the bed can be filled with fresh soil and provision made for correct drainage. It is surprising how much extra light can often be obtained by raising a bed a few feet above ground level. A raised bed can be planted in the ordinary way with shrubs, herbaceous perennials and annuals, or it can be devoted to alpine and dwarf plants whose charms are most appreciated close to (see p.58 for suggestions).

Perhaps the quickest, though not necessarily the cheapest, solution for difficult and dark places is to use containers (see p.59). As well as being decorative in their own right, these broaden the scope and enable one to grow plants which might otherwise fail in such adverse conditions.

(In addition to the suggestions below, see *Euonymus*, *Gaultheria Ribes*, *Sarcococca*.)

Shrubs

Aucuba

A medium-sized evergreen shrub 6–10 ft (1.8–3 m) high, *A. japonica* has leaves either dark green, variegated or spotted with yellow, depending on the form. 'Crotonifolia' has handsome golden-variegated leaves. Female plants produce attractive red berries in winter, if grown with males. The aucuba succeeds in dense and dry shade and is excellent in town gardens.

Buxus

The common box, *B. sempervirens*, will tolerate deep shade and makes a useful evergreen shrub or hedge, thriving on chalky soils. There are numerous cultivars, ranging in size from dwarf to large and some having variegated or coloured foliage. They include the tall 'Handsworthensis', with thick, dark green leaves, and the popular 'Gold Tip', with yellow-tipped leaves (see p.61).

Choisya

The Mexican orange blossom, *C. ternata*, is a most versatile evergreen shrub, equally at home in sun or shade, although less so under trees. Of rounded bushy habit, it grows 8–10 ft (2.5–3 m) high and bears clusters of fragrant white blossom in April and May, sometimes continuing until October. It is also extremely hardy.

× *Fatshedera lizei*

This hybrid between *Fatsia japonica* and ivy (probably the Irish ivy, *Hedera helix* 'Hibernica') is a handsome evergreen shrub or semi-climber up to 10 ft (3 m), with large, leathery, lustrous, dark green leaves like those of the ivy. It is a tough and vigorous plant, invaluable for dense dry shade, especially in towns. It usually

Above: the rose of Sharon, *Hypericum calycinum* (left), is an invaluable groundcover; *Ilex aquifolium* 'Silver Milkboy' (right), an attractive variegated holly

Below: the Oregon grape, *Mahonia aquifolium* (left), an outstanding shrub for shade; *Skimmia japonica* (right) contributes interest for much of the year

needs supporting with a stake, but can be kept more bushy by pinching out when young.

Fatsia

Well known as a houseplant, *F. japonica*, may grow 6–10 ft (1.8–3 m) high and has huge, lobed, shiny, dark green leaves and, in autumn, rounded heads of milky white flowers. It is a striking evergreen for a sheltered spot in shade.

Hedera

The familiar ivies are invaluable evergreen climbers or groundcover for dark spots, particularly in town gardens. The common ivy, *H. helix*, will succeed in almost any situation and soil, rapidly clothing a shady wall or carpeting bare ground where little else would survive. Many forms are available, with plain green, variegated or variously coloured leaves of different shapes.

Hypericum

The rose of Sharon, *H. calycinum*, is a vigorous, widespreading, low shrub, no more than 1–1½ ft (30–45 cm) high, with masses of golden yellow flowers from June to September. It is an ideal groundcover, even in full shade and dry soil. Once established, it is best cut back to near ground level in February each year to keep it compact (see p.15). The tutsan, *H. androsaemum*, is another useful member of the genus for dry shady places. Only 2–3 ft (60–90 cm) high and across, it has large deciduous leaves, small yellow flowers from June to September and black fruits. It seems indifferent to soil conditions and seeds itself with abandon.

Ilex

With its dark green, prickly leaves, dense pyramidal habit and red berries in winter (if male and female plants are grown together), the common holly, *I. aquifolium*, is one of the best evergreens. It is quite happy in heavy shade, although berrying less freely, and may be grown as a small tree, reaching a height of 30–40 ft (9–12 m) and with a spread of some 20 ft (6 m), or used to form a hedge. It does not take kindly to transplanting and is most succesful from self- sown seed. There are a large number of cultivars of different habits, leaf shapes and colours. Many of them are variegated (see p.15), although some of these are inclined to revert.

Lonicera

Of the shrubby honeysuckles, the semi-evergreen *L. pileata* is a fine groundcover plant, particularly for shady banks and dry areas. Only about 3 ft (90 cm) high and spreading, its main attraction is the neat, dark green, shining foliage, although insignificant whitish flowers appear in May, sometimes followed by violet berries.

Mahonia

The Oregon grape, *M. aquifolium*, is a small evergreen shrub 3–5 ft (90 cm–1.5 m) high and as wide, which covers the ground by means of suckers.It should be cut back in spring, just after flowering, to stop it becoming straggly. The glossy, dark green leaves, made up of leaflets, turn purplish red in winter, while the rich yellow flowers may start to open in February, reaching a peak in April and May. Abundant blue-black berries are also produced. This attractive plant is not fussy about soil or situation and will do well in all but the densest shade (see p.15).

Pachysandra

The evergreen *P. terminalis* is a semi-woody plant, less than 1 ft (30 cm) high. It is an efficient carpeter in shade, developing into a solid low mass, and has unusual diamond-shaped leaves of light green, with inconspicuous flowers in spring. It tolerates dry soil, but is not good on chalk.

Prunus

The cherry laurel or common laurel, *P. laurocerasus*, is one of the most shade-tolerant evergreens and will thrive in almost any soil. The dwarf forms, such as 'Otto Luyken', 'Schipkaensis' and 'Zabeliana' are all about 3 ft (90 cm) high, with a spread of 5 ft (1.5 m) or more, and can be recommended as groundcover. They have narrow, shining green leaves and spikes of small white flowers in spring.

Rubus

Although not outstandingly ornamental in flower, several members of this genus (which includes the raspberry and blackberry) are good ground-covering plants for sun or shade. Especially useful for a dry shady place and very fast growing is the semi-evergreen *R. tricolor*. It is about 1 ft (30 cm) high, with long, trailing, bristly stems and dark green leaves, felted white beneath. Solitary white flowers appear in July and are followed by bright red fruits, which are worth eating.

Ruscus

Butcher's broom, *R. aculeatus*, is a small evergreen shrub 2–3 ft (60–90 cm) high, spreading by suckers and making thick clumps. It bears bright red berries, if male and female are grown together, and is an indispensable plant for deep shade and poor conditions.

Sambucus

The native common elder, *S. nigra*, is easily recognized in the countryside by the heads of scented creamy flowers in June and later the heavy bunches of shiny black fruits (both of which are used to make wine). A deciduous shrub or tree some 15–30 ft (4.5–9 m) tall, it is often considered a weed in gardens because of its propensity to reproduce itself from seed. However, it is a real utility plant for difficult sites and will grow in damp dark corners and on extremely chalky soils.

Skimmia

The adaptable *S. japonica* will flourish in various degrees of shade, in dry conditions and on acid or alkaline soil. It is a compact evergreen bush, 3–4 ft (90 cm–1.2 m) high and the same width. The fragrant white blossom in April and May is succeeded by round, bright red fruits (when male and female plants are grouped), which persist through the winter (see p.15).

Symphoricarpus

The snowberry, *S. albus* var. *laevigatus (S. rivularis)*, is a vigorous suckering shrub 4–5 ft (1.2–1.5 m) high. Its chief merit is the large, pure white berries, which are freely carried from October into the new year and add a touch of brightness to the winter months. It is a popular choice for dark out-of-the-way places in the garden, where its rampant growth will not cause trouble. It forms dense thickets and, although deciduous, can be an effective screen.

Taxus

The English yew, *T. baccata*, with its small, narrow, dark green leaves and red fruits on female plants, is a useful evergreen for shady conditions. It is usually seen as a tree some 40 ft (12 m) tall or as a formal clipped hedge, but there are numerous cultivars of varying habits and foliage colours. They include some low prostrate kinds, like 'Repandens', which are superb groundcover for deep shade. The yew is suitable for almost any type of reasonably drained soil.

Viburnum

The laurustinus, *V. tinus*, is a deservedly popular evergreen shrub, with masses of dark green, glossy foliage and a long succession of pink-budded white flowers in flat heads from November to April. 'Eve Price' is a delightful form with pinkish blooms. Growing about 8–10 ft (2.5–3 m) high, it is a multi-purpose plant for sun or shade, although flowering less freely in very dense shade. It may also be used as a screen.

Vinca

Few plants are so accommodating and decorative as the periwinkles, both of them first-class groundcover for steep banks, waste ground and other awkward situations in shade and excellent for town gardens. The greater periwinkle, *V. major*, is a rampant trailing shrub and roots as it spreads. It has dark green leaves, or leaves boldly edged in creamy white in the often seen 'Variegata', and bright blue flowers opening in April, sometimes continuing at odd times until September. The lesser periwinkle, *V. minor*, is similar, but smaller and neater, making a low thick carpet. Neither flower as well in shade, but the mats of evergreen foliage are ample compensation.

Perennials

Asplenium

The hart's tongue fern, *A. scolopendrium* (*Phyllitis scolopendrium*) is a native evergreen fern with bright green, broad, strap-shaped fronds, 1–2 ft (60–90 cm) tall. It revels in shade, reproducing itself readily, and will grow in any soil, including chalk, but must have some moisture (see p.20).

Convallaria

The lily of the valley, *C. majalis*, is an unpredictable yet highly desirable plant, with the gracefully hanging, scented, white, bell-shaped flowers in spring set off by fresh green foliage. It seems to

The hart's tongue fern, *Asplenium scolopendrium*, is distinctive for its undulating fronds

thrive in many different soils, even in town gardens, preferring shade or half-shade. Once established, it is a vigorous spreader and, as the leaves last until autumn, it makes an efficient ground-cover about 9 in. (23 cm) high.

Dryopteris

The common native fern, *D. filix-mas*, known as the male fern, grows wild in all sorts of unlikely places and happily accepts both dry impoverished ground and heavy shade. It unfolds into large, dull green, divided fronds of elegant upright habit, eventually reaching a height of 4 ft (1.2 m), and soon colonizes the surrounding soil.

Euphorbia

A low evergreen perennial about 2 ft (60 cm) high, *E. robbiae* has rosettes of dark green leaves on purplish stems and greenish yellow flowers in spring. With its creeping roots, it is a reliable and quick groundcover for poor shady spots.

Iris

The long-suffering *I. foetidissima*, stinking gladwyn, will withstand deep shade and dry soil of any kind, though doing best in a moist well-drained position. Growing to some 1½ ft (45 cm) high, it forms clumps of rich green, arching, evergreen leaves, with bluish lilac flowers in early summer, followed by striking orange seed heads. These last into winter and are good for cutting. 'Citrina' is an improved form, with larger yellow flowers and bigger seed pods.

Saxifraga

The familiar London pride, *S. × urbium*, has rosettes of spoon-shaped leaves, from which arise loose panicles of starry pink flowers on 1 ft (30 cm) stems in early summer. It is a compact groundcover for permanently shady areas, provided the soil is moist, and good in town gardens, as the name implies.

Waldsteinia ternata, a delightful evergreen carpeter for heavy shade

Symphytum

The ground-covering comfrey, *S. grandiflorum*, is a rapid spreader no more than 10 in. (25 cm) high. It develops into a close mat of foliage, producing pale yellow, tubular flowers in spring. It likes shade and does best in a moist heavy soil, but will also cope with relatively dry conditions.

Trachystemon

Another member of the borage family, as is comfrey, *T. orientale* is a vigorous perennial for any shady place large enough to contain it. The huge, hairy, heart-shaped leaves emerge in late spring and are preceded by purplish blue flowers, the overall height being 1–1½ ft (30–45 cm) and the width 2 ft (60 cm).

Waldsteinia

The pretty little *W. ternata* creates thick mats of evergreen strawberry foliage and has golden yellow blooms in April and May. It is content with dry or moist soil, sun or shade, and is restrained enough for the town garden (see p.21).

A NORTH-FACING BORDER

A border facing north and cut off from the sun by intervening obstacles comes under the general heading of permanent shade, except perhaps briefly in midsummer when the sun is highest. However, because of its open aspect, the shade is usually less oppressive than in a dark enclosed area, although this depends on the height and proximity of any buildings or trees. It is often a bleak site, but can be improved by providing shelter in the form of a hedge or screen. The plants already mentioned under permanent shade (pp.13–22) will, of course, do equally well here; and for further suggestions, see *Chaenomeles, Cotoneaster, Garrya, Pyracantha, Rosa* in the next section.

Shrubs

Camellia

The innumerable cultivars of the common camellia, *C. japonica*, are prized not only for their magnificent flowers, from early to late spring, but also for their highly polished, evergreen leaves, which remain decorative all year. Most are medium-sized shrubs 10–12 ft (3–3.5 m) high, although they may become much larger with age. Those with a more compact habit of growth are ideal as free-standing specimens in a north-facing position. This gives protection from early morning sunshine, which can damage the blooms after frost by causing them to thaw too rapidly. Camellias do particularly well in town gardens, where there is less exposure to wind and the risk of frost damage is reduced. Two well-tried favourites are 'Adolphe Audusson' – blood-red semi-double flowers with prominent gold stamens; and 'Alba Plena' – large, double, white flowers on a bushy plant.

The common camellia needs fairly high summer temperatures in order to form buds and for this reason does not succeed in Scotland. A better choice in colder districts are the many *C. × williamsii* hybrids, which flower profusely over a long period, from November to May, and have the added merit of shedding the dead blooms. These include the famous 'Donation' – erect and vigorous, with semi-double, silvery pink flowers in March and April; and 'St Ewe' – single, funnel-shaped, purplish pink flowers and neat upright habit.

All camellias require moist lime-free soil containing peat or leafmould and benefit from regular mulching.

Osmanthus

An evergreen shrub which slowly attains a height of 6–10 ft (1.8–3 m), *O. × burkwoodii* has dark, shining green leaves and clusters of sweet-smelling white flowers in April or May. The holly-like *O. heterophyllus* is a dense bush of similar height, with fragrant white flowers in autumn; there is also a form with variegated leaves. These attractive shrubs make good thick hedges, if required, and are content with shade and a wide range of soils, including shallow chalk.

Paeonia

The shrubby peonies are such magnificent foliage and flowering plants that they amply repay a little extra care. Although perfectly hardy, they need protection from spring frosts, which can damage the young shoots and buds; at the same time, they should not have too warm a position, which would encourage premature growth. A north-facing situation is therefore ideal, with a screen of sacking, if necessary, to shelter them from frost. They do best in a rich, well drained soil.

A deciduous shrub, *P. delavayi* attains a height of 5–6 ft (1.5–1.8 m) and produces deep crimson, cup-shaped flowers with prominent golden anthers in May or June. Its greatest attribute,

Left: the gorgeous blooms of the tree peony, derived from *Paeonia suffruticosa*

Right: *Ribes sanguineum* 'Brocklebankii', a flowering currant with golden yellow foliage

however, is the large, deeply divided, dark green foliage. The same may be said of *P. lutea* var. *ludlowii*, a handsome plant of similar dimensions, whose leaves tend to obscure the golden yellow, saucer-shaped blooms. The many forms of the tree peony, *P. suffruticosa*, grow 4–5 ft (1.2–1.5 m) high and bring an exotic touch to any garden. Enormous single, semi-double or double flowers are borne from late May in a range of colours from white to crimson-purple. (See also p.28 for herbaceous peonies.)

Prunus

As well as the cherry laurel, *P. laurocerasus* (p.17), the Portugal laurel, *P. lusitanica*, is a fine evergreen for growing in shade. It may be allowed to develop into a stately shrub, reaching 15–20 ft (4.5–6 m) high and 12–15 ft (3.5–4.5 m) wide, or can be trained into formal shape or as a hedge. The abundant racemes of scented white blossom in June are shown off by rich green, glossy foliage and followed by small, dark purple fruits. It thrives on all soils.

Ribes

The mountain currant, *R. alpinum*, is very tolerant of shade and not fussy about soil. It is a neat deciduous shrub, some 6–9 ft (1.8–3 m) tall and as much in diameter, with modest, greenish yellow flowers in spring and red berries; the leaves turn yellow in autumn. 'Brocklebankii', a cultivar of the popular flowering currant, *R. sanguineum*, demands a shady place for the sake of its yellow foliage, which tends to burn in full sun. It is a pleasant low-growing shrub, 4–5 ft (1.2–5 m) high, and produces pink flowers in April. The currants are good in town gardens.

Sarcococca

The sarcococcas, relatives of box, provide excellent evergreen groundcover, particularly in the small garden, where their low compact growth is appreciated. About 2 ft (90 cm) high and wide, *S. hookeriana* var. *digyna* has glossy, dark green leaves, white fragrant flowers in winter and black fruits. The similar but dwarfer *S. humilis* suckers to form clumps and bears pinky white flowers in February. Both withstand shade and dry soil.

Viburnum

Another evergreen viburnum suitable for shade, apart from *V. tinus* (p.19), is *V. davidii*, although it is not successful under trees. This wide mound-shaped shrub grows 2–3 ft (60–90 cm) in height and 4–5 ft (1.2–1.5 m) in spread and in June carries flat heads of small white flowers against the dark green, veined leaves. Turquoise-blue berries are produced, if male and female plants are grouped.

Aconitum

The monkshoods, mainly hybrids between *A. napellus* and *A. variegatum*, are stately herbaceous perennials up to 4 ft (1.2 m) tall, with stiff spires of helmeted flowers and glossy, dark green, divided leaves. Blooming in various tones of blue from July to September, they do as well in shade as in full sun. The roots are highly poisonous.

Perennials

Anemone

The Japanese anemone, *A.* × *hybrida* (*A. japonica* of gardens), is a beautiful perennial for the shady border and does well in town gardens. It multiplies freely once established, does not need staking, despite its height of 2–3 ft (60–90 cm), and flowers at a welcome time in early autumn. The blooms are a delicate rose-pink, although there are several named kinds, ranging from white to pale to deep pink and with semi-double or double flowers (see p.26).

Above: the Japanese anemone, *Anemone* x *hybrida* (left), an old favourite in gardens; *Bergenia crassifolia* (right), with handsome spoon-shaped leaves

Below: *Helleborus corsicus* (left) flowers early in the year; the double red peony, *Paeonia officinalis* 'Rubra Plena' (right), has been grown since the sixteenth century

Bergenia

The bergenia species and hybrids offer a rich variety of colours in their large rounded leaves, which in some cases remain a fresh green and in others assume pink, purple or red tints in winter. Low-growing perennials usually around 1 ft (30 cm) high, they carpet the ground by means of creeping rhizomes and are invaluable for shady areas. They flourish in all except waterlogged or very light soils. As a bonus to the bold evergreen foliage, they have dense heads of purple, mauve or pink flowers on red stems in March or April. Among those which can be recommended are *B. cordifolia* 'Purpurea'; *B. crassifolia*; *B.* 'Abendglut', 'Ballawley', 'Silberlicht' and 'Sunningdale'.

Helleborus

For brightening up the garden in winter and early spring, there are few plants to surpass the hellebores. Most of them actively prefer shade and are not particular about the soil, as long as it is not too dry. None grow more than 2 ft (60 cm) tall. The Lenten roses, *H. orientalis* and its progeny, are probably the best known, with nodding bowl-shaped flowers of cream, white, purple, pink or crimson, often spotted inside and flushed with green. Another deciduous hellebore, *H. atrorubens*, has unusual plum-purple blooms with yellow anthers and is a lovely sight in late January. The evergreen *H. corsicus* is notable for the prickly blue-green foliage, forming a background to pale green, pendent cups. The native stinking hellebore, *H. foetidus*, is also worth growing, with its clump of deeply divided, dark green, evergreen leaves and bell-shaped flowers of light green edged with purple.

Hosta

Hostas are superb foliage plants for furnishing shady parts where the soil does not dry out. They look equally impressive in a natural woodland setting, in a formal border, or edging a patio in a town garden, and their usefulness is now appreciated by many gardeners. The leaves, in gradually spreading clumps, provide a striking architectural feature throughout late spring and summer and often again in autumn; they are supplemented by spikes of trumpet- or bell-shaped flowers in the summer. The average height of these robust perennials is 1½–2½ ft (45–75 cm). Unfortunately the foliage is enticing to slugs, which should be kept at bay with slug pellets, and rabbits can also cause damage.

The most widely available hostas include *H. crispula* – dark green, long, pointed leaves with broad, wavy, white margins and pale lilac flowers in June; *H. fortunei* 'Albopicta' – a flower arranger's favourite, having distinctive, pale yellowish foliage bordered with light green in May, maturing to soft green, and lavender flowers in July and August; *H. lancifolia* – shiny, dark green, narrow leaves and deep lilac blooms in September; *H. sieboldiana* var. *elegans* – huge blue-grey leaves, turning yellow in autumn, and dense lilac-white flowers in summer; *H.* 'Thomas Hogg' – similar to *H. crispula*, but larger leaves, with wider, creamy white edging, and pale mauve flowers; and *H. ventricosa* – a large grower, with glossy, rich green, heart-shaped foliage and lovely, deep violet blooms in July and August.

Paeonia

Although the herbaceous peonies are often thought of as sun-loving plants, some can be grown successfully in shade. They do well on chalk or any other kind of soil, so long as it is fertile and well drained. A notable example is *P. emodi*, which prefers shady conditions and grows about 3 ft (90 cm) high. Beautiful, pure white, fragrant flowers, with golden anthers, appear on arching stems in late spring and the smooth, dark green leaves prolong the interest through the summer. The old-fashioned double red peony, *P. officinalis* 'Rubra Plena', also gives full value in shade. Some 1½–2 ft (45–60 cm) high, it blooms in May and the foliage remains attractive until autumn (see p.26). (See also p.24 for shrubby peonies.)

Phlox

The numerous border phloxes descended from *P. paniculata* are tall plants to 4 ft (1.2 m) or more, with heavy pyramids of scented flowers at their peak in August. These come in a range of brilliant and softer colours, which are apt to burn in full sun. Phloxes are therefore better planted in a shady bed and require rich, not too dry soil.

A NORTH-FACING WALL OR FENCE

A wall or fence facing north may seem a daunting prospect to the gardener. However, by careful selection of plants, it can be transformed into an unusual feature and several climbers and wall shrubs are seen to advantage in such a situation. Fruits such as morello cherries, red and black currants, blackberries and loganberries also give good results when trained against a northerly wall. (For further details, see *The Fruit Garden Displayed*.)

Concerning the type of shade and other conditions, much the same remarks apply as for a north-facing border (see p.22). A number of shrubs are suitable for both positions, either free-standing in a border or supported by a wall or fence – for instance, chaenomeles, garrya and pyracantha. Most of those mentioned below are equally successful in an east-facing aspect, which could be described as part shade, receiving sun in the mornings only. The major caveat to this is the camellia, whose blooms will be injured if they thaw too quickly after frost. An alternative use for many of the true climbers, like *Hydrangea petiolaris* and honeysuckle, is to allow them to clamber into the branches of deciduous trees (see p.56). With especially vigorous ones, this is often more satisfactory than a wall, where they tend to grow to the top and leave the lower part bare. (For further suggestions, see *Choisya, Hedera.*)

Once again, thorough preparation of the soil is essential and particularly so near a wall, where the earth is often dry and impoverished.

Shrubs

Berberidopsis

The coral plant, *B. corallina*, is an evergreen climber to about 15 ft (4.5 m) high and 8 ft (2.5 m) wide, with dark green, spine-edged leaves. From July to September it is bedecked in gorgeous, deep red, globe-shaped flowers crowded in hanging clusters. A native of Chile, it is not completely hardy and should be given the protection of a wall, where it is sheltered both from strong sun and from cold drying winds. It requires a deep moist soil and dislikes limy conditions.

Camellia

Many camellias thrive in a north-facing position (see also p.22) and some of those with a more open habit are particularly suitable for training against a wall. Among *C. japonica* cultivars which may be singled out for the purpose are 'Lady Clare' – spreading, almost pendulous, with large semi-double rose-pink flowers; and 'Nagasaki' – vigorous, with semi-double carmine blooms spotted white. Of the *C.* × *williamsii* hybrids, there are 'Elegant Beauty' – arching, with deep rose, anemone-form flowers; and the outstanding 'J. C.Williams' – horizontal growth, with a profusion of single phlox-pink blooms. Perhaps the best of all, however, is 'Francie L.', an allied hybrid, which has large, semi-double, deep rose flowers and long dark leaves.

Chaenomeles

Familiarly known as "japonica", the various forms of *C. speciosa* are perfect for the small garden, happy in sun or shade, against a wall or in the open. Much-branched, spreading, deciduous shrubs, they are generally some 6 ft (1.8 m) tall and slightly less in width. They flower continuously from February or March to June and sometimes again in autumn, although blooming less freely in shade. 'Cardinalis' is an old cultivar with crimson-scarlet flowers, while 'Moerloosii' (sometimes incorrectly called 'Apple Blossom') has large white flowers suffused with pink and carmine; the dwarfer 'Simonii' has deep red semi-double blooms. The hybrids of *C. speciosa* grouped under the name *C. × superba* are lower-growing, mostly 3–4 ft (90 cm–1.2 m) high, and just as attractive. There is a choice of glowing colours, from the deep red with golden anthers of 'Crimson and Gold', to the orange-scarlet of 'Knap Hill Scarlet' and the brilliant crimson of 'Rowallane'.

Clematis

The numerous species and hybrids of clematis are deservedly among our most popular climbing shrubs. Although they revel in full sunshine, a surprising number of them will succeed against a north- or east-facing wall and all like to have their roots in shade. In many cases they preserve their colour better out of the sun. A good choice can be had from the hybrids which flower in spring and early summer, such as the well-known 'Bees' Jubilee' – blooms of mauve-pink with deep carmine bars; 'H. F. Young' – abundant, large, wedgwood-blue flowers with cream stamens; and 'Nelly Moser' – an old favourite, with huge, flat, pale pink blooms striped carmine (see p.33). Some of the later-flowering hybrids can also be tried, for instance, 'Comtesse de Bouchaud' – satiny rose blooms with cream stamens; 'Hagley Hybrid' – delicate shell-pink flowers; and the stalwart 'Jackmanii' – masses of purple flowers with green stamens.

Cotoneaster

The familiar *C. horizontalis* is an indispensable shrub for a north- or east-facing wall, making a neat herringbone pattern of branches up to 10 ft (3 m) high, thickly covered with tiny leaves. These turn rich orange and red in autumn, creating a pleasant picture with the abundant bright red berries, and do not fall until the new year. It may also be grown in the open, as a low spreading shrub, or used to cover a bank.

Chaenomeles x *superba* 'Knap Hill Scarlet' bears a profusion of flowers in spring and early summer

Euonymus

The versatile *E. fortunei* var. *radicans* is a creeping or trailing evergreen shrub, rooting at intervals from the long stems as they cover the ground or climb up a wall, where it may grow to a height of 20 ft (6 m) or more. The leaves are oval and dark green or, in the attractive form 'Variegatus', greyish green margined with white and occasionally tinged pink. It tolerates deep shade and succeeds in town gardens.

Garrya

A bushy shrub some 6–12 ft (1.8–3.5 m) high and as wide, *G. elliptica* is a fine evergreen for planting against a wall or fence or on its own. It appreciates a sheltered sunny spot with rather dry soil, but can be grown in shade. Male plants are more ornamental, having long, silvery grey catkins in winter.

Hydrangea

The climbing hydrangea, *H. petiolaris*, is invaluable for clothing large expanses of a north-facing wall and for growing into tall trees. It may also be used to cover old tree stumps. Clinging by means of aerial roots, it reaches a height of 50–70 ft (15–21 m) and produces a mass of flat flower heads in summer, consisting of small greenish white florets in the centre and larger white florets at the edges. It is deciduous.

Jasminum

The rambling angular branches of the winter jasmine, *J. nudiflorum*, are best supported by a wall or fence and, although it likes sun, it does not mind the shade of buildings. It grows 12–15 ft (3.5–4.5) high and is always a welcome sight in winter, when the starry, bright yellow flowers appear on leafless green stems. The long growths should be cut back immediately after flowering. It is also excellent planted at the top of a steep bank and allowed to hang down it.

Parthenocissus

A tendril-climbing vine 20–30 ft (6–9 m) tall, *P. henryana* is happiest grown against a north-facing wall, where the markings of the deciduous foliage are most apparent. The dark green or bronze leaves develop a silvery variegation on the veins before turning red in autumn.

Pyracantha

The firethorns or pyracanthas are undemanding evergreen shrubs, which may be planted in the open or, for greatest effect, against a wall. The one most frequently seen on house walls, *P. coccinea* 'Lalandei', has a height of 12–15 ft (3.5–4.5 m) and spread of 10–12 ft (3–3.5 m), with white hawthorn-like blossom in June, followed by orange-red berries in autumn and winter. The taller *P. atalantioides* is distinguished by its larger, dark green,

Left: the flowers of *Clematis* 'Nelly Moser' do not become bleached in shade

Right: the popular climbing rose 'Danse du Feu' may be grown on a wall or trained to a support

shining leaves and long-lasting scarlet fruits throughout the winter. More compact plants 8–10 ft (2.5–3 m) high are the thorny *P. rogersiana*, with small dainty leaves, lovely white flowers and plentiful reddish orange berries; and *P.* 'Watereri', which is very prolific in bright red fruits.

Rosa

Roses are essentially sun-loving and many gardeners might despair of being able to grow them in shade. However, there are a number of roses, mainly climbers, which have proved their worth in a north-facing situation.

The well-known 'Danse du Feu', one of the first of the modern repeat-flowering climbing roses, bears orange-scarlet double flowers throughout the summer and grows to around 12 ft (3.5 m). 'Maigold' lives up to its name with a display of very fragrant, bronze and yellow, semi-double blooms in May and sometimes flowers again in late summer. It is thorny, but has fine glossy foliage and may be grown either as a climber, to some 10 ft (3 m), or as a shrub, making a mounded bush 5 ft (1.5 m) high (see p.9). Another recurrent-flowering climber, 'Parkdirektor Riggers' produces blood-red semi-double flowers in abundance over a long period. It has dark green, shining leaves and reaches a height of 12–15 ft (3.5–4.5 m). The vigorous 'Hamburger Phoenix' also has a long season of bloom, from June onwards, with crimson semi-double flowers. The velvety, scarlet-black, scented, double flowers of 'Guinée' make an unusual contribution at the same time. On the other hand, 'Soldier Boy' flowers mainly at midsummer, with clusters of single scarlet-crimson blooms. Like most of the repeat-flowering climbers of restrained growth, it may be trained as a pillar rose and grown in a border if no wall space is available.

Many of the older roses have still not been superseded, although some have the disadvantage of only one flush of bloom. Dating from the early nineteenth century, 'Félicité Perpétue' is a strong rambler to 10 ft (3 m), with semi-evergreen leaves and rounded, fully double, creamy white flowers in July. It is excellent for clambering into an old fruit tree. The noisettes, a group of roses with clusters of distinctively perfumed flowers, were developed during the same period and named after their raiser. One of the few to survive is 'Madame Alfred Carrière', more akin to a modern climber in its ability to flower continuously from midsummer into autumn. A rampant grower which may attain 20 ft (6 m), it is ideal for covering a large wall and bears sweetly fragrant, whitish, pink-flushed, double flowers. The noisettes were later crossed with the tea-scented roses, the resulting hybrids combining the vigour and hardiness of the first with the colouring and scent of the second. A fine example of a climbing tea-noisette and a favourite of the Victorians, 'Gloire de Dijon' is richly perfumed and seldom out of flower after midsummer. The flat double blooms open buff and change to apricot and pink. Unfortunately only once-flowering, 'Madame Gregoire Staechelin' is equally vigorous and smothers itself in large, loose, double, rose-pink blooms, heavily scented, in June. Similarly, 'Paul's Lemon Pillar' gives a single burst of flower in June, with large, shapely, double blooms, of pale yellow fading to white, set off by large green leaves. 'Climbing Madame Caroline Testout', a climbing variety of an old hybrid tea rose, is more restrained at 8–10 ft (2.5–3 m) high, and very thorny, with double, warm pink flowers at midsummer, usually repeated in autumn.

Fragrant double flowers of an intense dark crimson in summer and autumn are the hallmark of 'Grüss an Teplitz'. This distinctive rose has strong arching shoots, 6–8 ft (1.8–2.5 m) high, and may be treated as a climber or kept as a large shrub by pruning. The hybrid perpetuals, a large class of roses which were very popular with the Victorians, have left us 'Hugh Dickson', with brilliant crimson, double flowers in summer. A lanky grower of great vigour, it is often seen with the long branches pegged down or bent over hoops and it may also be trained as a climber. 'Conrad Ferdinand Meyer', a robust descendant of *R. rugosa*, is best grown as a climber, otherwise making a gaunt shrub 8–10 ft (12.5–3 m) high. Large, full-petalled, silvery pink flowers, with a heady fragrance, appear in early summer and again in September.

Schizophragma

Closely allied and similar to the climbing hydrangea (p.32), *S. hydrangeoides* is a vigorous, self-clinging, deciduous climber, 30–40 ft (9–12 m) tall. It has flat heads of yellowish white flowers with heart-shaped yellow bracts in July and may be used in the same way as its relative.

PARTIAL SHADE

As the day progresses and the shadows change position, different parts of the garden become shaded. These will vary considerably according to the season and height of the sun.

Partial shade is the easiest type of shade to deal with, since so many plants appreciate protection from the full strength of the midday sun. The majority of plants already described would succeed, together with those recommended later for dappled shade (pp.41–53). The climbers and wall shrubs suitable for a north-facing wall (see p.28) are equally good on an east-facing one, with the important exception of camellias and rhododendrons, whose flowers might be harmed by the combination of frost and early morning sun, leading to rapid thawing. A westerly aspect offers particularly favourable conditions, as it is normally warm, sheltered and well supplied with moisture, and here the choice of plants is endless. A west-facing wall broadens the scope even further, offering shelter to many desirable shrubs which might otherwise be regarded as tender.

The list below is therefore confined to a selection of herbaceous perennials and annuals (given in that order) for a partially shady bed or border. For further recommendations, see *Anemone*, *Bergenia*, *Hosta*, *Phlox* (pp.25–8).

Perennials

Actaea

The baneberry, *A. rubra*, makes a good companion plant in the shade of shrubs and prefers a cool, fairly moist situation. Poisonous but attractive red berries are borne on spikes 1–1½ ft

The bugbane, *Cimicifuga racemosa*, does not need staking despite its height

(30–45 cm) long in early autumn, above green fern-like leaves. A very similar species, *A. spicata*, is distinguished by the glistening black fruits.

Alchemilla

With its lovely, greyish green leaves and delicate sprays of pale yellow flowers in early summer, *A. mollis* or lady's mantle enhances any mixed planting. About 1 ft (30 cm) high, it is amenable to sun or shade and spreads rapidly from self-sown seed. The flower heads can be cut off before the seeds ripen to keep it within bounds. It succeeds in town gardens and is beautiful in flower arrangements.

Aquilegia

The aquilegia long-spurred hybrids look particularly effective when massed among shrubs or herbaceous plants. They grow to about 2 ft (60 cm) and have attractive bluish grey foliage, with the columbine flowers in a great range of colours appearing in June and July. They seed themselves freely, but are best renewed regularly from bought seed, in order to preserve quality (see p.12).

Astrantia

The commonest species, *A. major*, is 1–2 ft (30–60 cm) high, with clumps of lobed leaves. In summer and autumn it produces unusual star-like flower heads, composed of greenish pink florets with a collar of bracts. It appreciates a moist soil.

Campanula

The cool blues, purples and whites of the bellflowers always seem appropriate in a shady border or woodland setting and they bring a breath of fresh air to town gardens. Some of them can be dangerously invasive, for instance *C. rapunculoides*, which spreads both by roots and by seed and should be avoided. However, *C. latifolia* is more easily controlled and makes clumps of rounded leaves, with 4 ft (1.2 m) stems carrying long funnel-shaped blue flowers in July; there is also a white form. Useful for its smaller stature is *C. glomerata* var. *dahurica*, which is some 1½ ft (45 cm) high and has wide violet-purple blooms.

Cimicifuga

The bugbane, *C. racemosa*, is an elegant border plant where the soil is sufficiently moist. Emerging from ferny foliage, the wand-like stalks reach 5–6 ft (1.5–1.8 m) and are topped with fluffy racemes of white flowers in July.

Dicentra

Known by various names such as bleeding heart, Dutchman's breeches and lady's locket, *D. spectabilis* is an old favourite in gardens. About 2 ft (60 cm) high, the gracefully arching stems are hung with rosy crimson heart-shaped buds opening in late spring, while the bluish green, finely cut leaves prolong the interest. It thrives in a position which is shaded during the hottest part of the day and does well in town gardens.

Gentiana

The willow gentian, *G. asclepiadea*, is a reliable plant for almost any situation and soil, although doing best in cool moist conditions. The arching stems, to 2ft (60 cm) high, are clad in willow-

Geranium himalayense, a beautiful example of the versatile cranesbills

like leaves and bear narrow bell-shaped flowers of rich blue in late summer.

Geranium

The cranesbills, members of the large genus *Geranium*, are among the most valuable hardy perennials, easily grown in all types of soil and often developing into dense groundcover. They can be recommended for town gardens. Many are tolerant of shade and some prefer it. To the first category belong *G. endressi* and its cultivars – vigorous clump-formers 1½ ft (45 cm) or more high, with handsome foliage and pink flowers continuously in summer; the slightly smaller *G. himalayense* (*G. grandiflorum*) – blue-purple veined blooms in July; and *G.* × *magnificum* – prolific violet-blue flowers in early summer.

In the second category, of definite shade-lovers, are *G. macrorrhizum* – an excellent carpeting plant about 1 ft (30 cm) high, with aromatic leaves and magenta, pink or white flowers according to the form, from May to July; mourning widow, *G. phaeum* – remarkable, very dark maroon flowers, varying to grey or white, in late spring, and the closely related *G. punctatum*; and *G. nodosum* – some 1½ ft (45 cm) high, with hummocks of glossy leaves and lilac flowers from spring into autumn, happy even in dry deep shade.

Viola

Many members of this extensive genus prefer cool shady conditions and a moist but well-drained soil. The vigorous *V. cornuta* forms clumps of small, rich green leaves and bears a profusion of lilac-purple, pale mauve or white flowers in spring. If these are then cut over, it will give a second crop in autumn. The hybrid V. 'Huntercombe Purple' has similar requirements, with large, deep purple blooms in spring and summer. Succeeding in dense shade or sun, *V. labradorica* is a scentless violet with purple-flushed foliage and lavender-blue flowers. It runs freely underground and can be a nuisance (see p.62). (See also p.40 for pansies).

Annuals

Asperula

The annual woodruff, *A. orientalis*, is a hardy annual no more than 1 ft (30 cm) tall, with fragrant, pale blue, tubular flowers in summer. It may be sown outside from March to May and will perform well in a shady bed or border.

Begonia

Some of the most popular and versatile summer bedding plants are the wax begonias derived from *B. semperflorens*. Of bushy habit and usually under 1 ft (30 cm) high, they come in a variety of colours and often have bronze or purple leaves. They need warmth to raise from seed, but are widely available as plants from garden centres.

Collinsia

A hardy annual for a moist shady spot, *C. heterophylla* (*C. bicolor*) attains a height of 2 ft (60 cm) and produces two-lipped blooms of white and lilac or purple from June to September. It should be sown in the open in March or April.

Cynoglossum

The hound's tongue, *C. amabile*, is a biennial which succeeds when treated as an annual, sown in March and April. Growing

1½–2 ft (45–60 cm), it has grey-green leaves and turquoise-blue flowers in summer.

Digitalis

The wild foxglove, *D. purpurea*, has been largely replaced in gardens by cultivars with white, pink or apricot flowers. Stately plants some 4 ft (1.2 m) high, they are normally biennial and easily raised from seed sown in spring. They will grow almost anywhere, but look most at home in informal surroundings.

Impatiens

A hardy annual to 6½ ft (2 m) tall, *I. glandulifera* bears clusters of long purple flowers in early autumn. It self-sows freely and has become naturalized in parts of Britain.

The numerous busy lizzies, descended from *I. walleriana*, are usually grown as half-hardy annuals and will bloom all through the summer in sun or shade.

Lobelia

The many named forms of *L. erinus*, with flowers of violet or white as well as deep blue, are indispensable edging plants. They are generally sown under glass in February, for planting out in May.

Nemophila

Baby blue eyes, *N. menziesii*, is a hardy annual about 6 in. (15 cm) high, with feathery foliage and charming sky-blue flowers with white centres from June onwards.

Nicotiana

Various species of *Nicotiana* have contributed to the evolution of the modern tobacco plants, in a range of colours from crimson and mauve to lime-green and white. In some, the trumpet-shaped blooms open at dusk and are powerfully scented, in others the flowers remain open by day but are less fragrant. They vary in height from 3 ft (90 cm) to 1½ ft (45 cm). Seed may be sown under glass as late as April and all will be content in a shady position.

Viola

Pansies grown as half-hardy annuals, from seed sown in spring to flower in the summer, are a delightful addition to a shady border. There are many different colours from which to choose.

DAPPLED SHADE

Dappled shade is produced by deciduous trees whose height, shape and type of leaf allow sunshine to filter through the canopy – for example, ash, silver birch, larch, paperbark maple and rowan. Many plants enjoy these conditions, in which they experience continuous light shade during the summer and are never in direct sun. The one serious snag is that they are deprived of much of the moisture and food essential to their welfare by the roots of the trees. Birch has such hungry roots that, even if one attempts to improve the soil for the sake of the plants beneath, the tree itself will probably benefit most.

Despite these disadvantages, dappled shade gives scope for varied and interesting planting at all levels, from shrubs to perennials and bulbs. A large number of plants, including rhododendrons, lilies and primulas, appreciate the broken light provided by trees and associate well to create an impression of natural woodland. In addition to these, most of the plants already recommended are worth trying in dappled shade and some, for instance, hellebores, lilies of the valley, aquilegias, campanulas and ferns, are particularly appropriate in an informal setting.

Lilies, like the lovely yellow *Lilium szovitsianum*, revel in dappled shade

Shrubs

Arctostaphylos

The bearberry, *A. uva-ursi*, is a prostrate trailing evergreen and covers the ground with masses of dark green foliage, sometimes becoming purplish in winter. Tiny white or pink urn-shaped flowers appear in April, giving way to red berries. Together with the very similar *A. nevadensis*, it prefers a lime-free soil and is a useful carpet under rhododendrons and other shrubs. It is also good for clothing dry shady banks.

Camellia

Camellias (see p.22) lend themselves to a natural woodland site, where the canopy is high and the shade not too dense. They are excellent with rhododendrons and share their soil requirements.

Daphne

The spurge laurel, *D. laureola*, is a bushy shrub up to 4 ft (1.2 m) high, with shining, dark, evergreen leaves and rather insignificant, yellowish green blossom in early spring. The slightly taller *D. pontica* produces a profusion of fragrant flowers in April. Both are useful woodlanders, liking a moist peaty soil.

Gaultheria

The creeping wintergreen, *G. procumbens*, is an attractive evergreen carpeter 2–6 in. (5–15 cm) high, with tufts of shining, dark green leaves and white bell-shaped flowers in summer, followed by bright red fruits. It is ideal for covering the ground beneath shrubs. The more rampant salal, *G. shallon*, forms thickets about 4 ft (1.2 m) high and across. It has tough, leathery, evergreen leaves and clusters of pinkish white flowers giving way to dark purple fruits. Its invasive tendency may be controlled by cutting back in early spring. Gaultherias are best in moist lime-free soils containing peat or leafmould, but will tolerate dry conditions.

Linnaea

The twinflower, *L. borealis*, is a diminutive, mat-forming, evergreen shrub, with pinkish white funnel-shaped flowers in summer. The variety *americana* is stronger and more satisfactory in gardens. It needs lime-free soil, but does not object if this is dry.

Mahonia

One of the finest of all evergreen shrubs, *M. japonica* grows some 7 ft (2 m) high and bears long drooping clusters of fragrant yellow flowers from winter to early spring, against a background of large, glossy, deep green, pinnate leaves. The hybrid *M.* 'Charity', flowering in November and December, is in the same class, but has upright or spreading flowers of a more intense yellow. Both flourish in quite heavy shade beneath trees, their foliage making an impressive foil for other plants, and are happy on all soils.

Rhododendron

The vast genus *Rhododendron* numbers hundreds of species and thousands of hybrids, the majority of which – in particular the well-known large-leaved kinds – are woodland plants par excellence. A high tree canopy not only supplies the cool shady conditions they prefer; it also helps to give protection against late frosts, which might kill the flowers, and to provide shelter from drying winds. However, all rhododendrons are moisture-lovers and surface-rooting and will not withstand competition from greedy trees like beech, birch or sycamore. For this reason, thin oak woodland is often recommended as the best place for rhododendrons, since the roots of the oaks are deep enough not to compete, while their leaves admit sufficient light. An acid soil (preferably pH 5) is essential, with peat and leafmould incorporated, and it should be moist but well drained. The following is just a small selection of some of the most dependable species and hybrids, all of them evergreen.

A dense shrub some 8 ft (2.5 m) high and 5 ft (1.5 m) across, *R. bureavii* has a coating of rusty red hairs on the undersurface of the leaves, with silvery young growths and rose-pink flowers in April and May. Slightly larger, yet bushy and compact, *R. wardii* produces saucer-shaped yellow blooms in May, thus escaping any risk of frost damage; it is important to choose a good form of this variable species. Growing as tall as 20 ft (6 m), *R. rex* has huge leaves, grey underneath, and large trusses of pink flowers in April and May. It succeeds in cold districts. The earlier flowering *R. fulvum*, about 15 ft (4.5 m) high, opens its pale pink blooms in March. The foliage is a polished dark green, with orange-brown felt beneath. The diminutive *R. ciliatum*, 4 ft (1.2 m) in height and spread, also flowers in March, with bell-shaped bluish pink blooms, and benefits from overhead protection.

One of the most famous hybrids, Naomi grows to about 15 ft (4.5 m) and has large clusters of fragrant, yellow-tinged, lilac flowers in May. There are several fine clones such as 'Exbury

Naomi'. Of similar height and exceptionally vigorous and free-flowering, 'Loderi King George' bears large, scented, pink to white blooms in May. It is a definite woodlander, needing shelter and shade. Also best in shade, since the flowers tend to burn in open sunshine, is 'Mrs G. W. Leak'. It grows to some 10 ft (3 m) and has widely funnel-shaped flowers, pink with a dark eye. Another medium-sized plant, Vanessa carries soft pink flowers in June, while the clone 'Vanessa Pastel' had cream pink-flushed blooms. The 12 ft (3.5 m) high Azor is valuable for its late flowering, in June and July, the trumpet-shaped blooms being salmon pink. For the small garden, few can compete with Elizabeth, a delightful spreading shrub only 5 ft (1.5 m) tall, with blood-red flowers in April. Finally, the evergreen azalea 'John Cairns', less than 3 ft (90 cm) in height, has dark orange-red flowers in May.

Stranvaesia

Although it is a rather gaunt-looking shrub or small tree, 20–30 ft (6–9 m) tall, *S. davidiana* is a valuable screening plant for a shady spot. It is a handsome sight in autumn, when some of the dark green leaves turn bright red and the branches are hung with bunches of brilliant crimson fruits.

Vaccinium

The native cowberry, *V. vitis-idaea*, is an excellent underplanting for rhododendrons and shares their soil and cultivation requirements. A low carpeting shrub, it forms neat tufts of evergreen box-like foliage, developing bronze tints in winter. The pinkish bell-shaped flowers in early summer are succeeded by dark red berries. It tolerates dry soil.

Xanthorhiza

An interesting deciduous shrub 2–3 ft (60–90 cm) high, the yellow-root, *X. simplicissima*, is valued mainly for the handsome divided and lobed leaves on erect stems. These turn bronzy purple in autumn and panicles of tiny purple flowers are borne in March and April. It spreads freely by suckers in any reasonable soil, but dislikes chalk.

Opposite above: the well-known Elizabeth, a small growing rhododendron with large flowers

Below: *Xanthorhiza simplicissima* is an uncommon but striking foliage shrub

Perennials

Ajuga

In the wild, the bugle, *A. reptans*, is found in woodland glades and clearings, carpeting the ground with small, oval, evergreen leaves and, in early summer, with blue flowers on upright shoots. There are several coloured-leaved forms, such as 'Atropurpurea' – purple foliage; 'Multicolor' – bronze, pink and yellow; and 'Variegata' – grey-green and cream (see p.48). It prefers a moist position.

Arisarum

The mouse plant, *A. proboscideum*, makes an interesting groundcover for dappled shade and a fairly moist soil. Among the shiny green spear-shaped leaves are hidden whitish flowers, with long protruding tails like those of mice. The foliage dies down by July (see p.48).

Aruncus

The goat's beard, *A. dioicus (A. sylvester, Spiraea aruncus)* is a superb herbaceous plant up to 5 ft (1.5 m) in height, with decorative fern-like leaves and great feathery plumes of creamy white blossom in June. The cultivar 'Kneiffei' is a miniature version with finely cut leaves. They are often recommended for a moist spot, but are content with any soil, in shade or sun (see p.11).

Athyrium

The lady fern, *A. felix-femina*, flourishes in shade and, although best in moist humus-rich soil, it will put up with dry conditions. The light green, lacy fronds unfold in late spring and reach some 2 ft (60 cm) high, before dying back in September. It sows itself readily.

Blechnum

The native hard fern, *B. spicant*, is an excellent plant for moist woodland, where it forms increasing clumps of glossy, dark green fronds, above which rise taller, slender, fertile fronds 1–1½ ft (30–45 cm) high. It is evergreen and will tolerate dry soil so long as this is lime-free.

Brunnera

A good strong-growing groundcover some 1½ ft (45 cm) high,

Winter aconites and *Cyclamen coum* are a charming combination in early spring

B. macrophylla has large heart-shaped leaves and blue forget-me-not flowers from April to June. The foliage, particularly in the form 'Variegata', is apt to scorch unless the plant is given a sheltered shady situation in a moisture-retentive soil.

Cornus

The creeping dogwood, *C. canadensis* (*Chamaepericlymenum canadense*) is a semi-herbaceous plant some 6 in. (15 cm) high, with underground shoots which rapidly colonize the ground. Lovely white flowers, consisting of four bracts, appear in May and June and the leaves turn reddish purple in autumn. It is happy in acid, fairly moist, woodland conditions.

Cyclamen

A great favourite for massing under trees, *C. hederifolium* produces its dainty pink, white or mauve flowers at a most welcome time of year, from September to November. In addition, the foliage remains attractive throughout the winter – a deep green with lovely silver mottling. This is probably the easiest species to grow, in any type of soil, and spreads from self-sown seed. It has the remarkable advantage that it will thrive even in the

Above: *Ajuga reptans* 'Variegata' (left), a useful variegated bugle for groundcover; the mouse plant, *Arisarum proboscideum* (right), always fascinates children

Below: *Lamium maculatum* and its form 'Beacon Silver', in front, which also succeeds in shade

deep shade of yew or cedar. The dwarfer *C. coum*, some 3 in. (7.5 cm) high, is another amenable species, with carmine flowers from January to March and dark red undersurfaces to the leaves (see p.47).

Dicentra

Succeeding in a cool shady position, *D. formosa* produces 1½ ft (45 cm) stems with locket-like pink or red flowers in May and June, dangling above delicate ferny leaves. It spreads by means of suckers. The popular 'Bountiful' has deep mauve-pink flowers.

Epimedium

Valued chiefly for their foliage effect, these perennials have the bonus of charming spurred flowers on airy stems in spring. All about 1 ft (30 cm) high, they gently colonize the ground once established and are perfectly happy even in dry shade. Perhaps the most attractive is the evergreen *E. perralderianum*, with bright green spiny-edged leaves, turning coppery bronze in autumn, and yellow flowers. The red-tinged leaves of *E. × rubrum* later become orange and yellow and the flowers are crimson. Flowering in May, *E. × versicolor* 'Sulphureum' has yellow blooms and copper-tinted foliage. All are good in town gardens.

Galax

A low-growing plant, forming hummocks of rounded, shiny, dark green leaves, *G. aphylla* (*G. urceolata*) sends up spikes of white flowers in summer. The evergreen foliage is bronzy in winter. It does best in dappled shade in lime-free soil.

Galium

The sweet woodruff, *G. odoratum*, is better known as *Asperula odorata*. Only 4–6 in. (10–15 cm) high, it rapidly develops into dense drifts of whorled foliage, with heads of scented, pure white flowers from May to July.

Lamium

A fast and efficient colonizer where the soil is sufficiently moist and cool, *L. maculatum* has dark green leaves with a white stripe and flowers of magenta, pink or white. It can be recommended for town gardens.

Lilium

It is not surprising that such an extensive genus as *Lilium* should contain both sun- and shade-lovers. While many demand as much sun as possible, some prefer light overhead shade, or partial shade, especially during the hottest part of the day. Others, for instance *L. martagon* and *L. pardalinum*, are quite adaptable to full sun or shade. The one prerequisite for all is perfect drainage and the majority do best on lime-free soil with leafmould or peat added.

In fact, most lilies appreciate coolness and shade at the roots and shelter from wind. They grow well in company with shrubs or herbaceous plants and seem more at home in natural surroundings, where they can spread freely, than in a formal flowerbed. Ideal for growing up through shrubs is *L. auratum*, 4–8 ft (1.2–2.5 m) tall and bearing huge bowl-shaped flowers, white with a golden ray and deep purple spots. However, because of its late flowering, in August and September, it is less successful in the north, unless grown in a pot (see p.61). Of similar height but blooming slightly earlier, *L. superbum* is a good woodland species, with recurved orange flowers, deepening to crimson at the base and maroon-spotted. The martagon lily, *L. martagon*, has become naturalized in Britain and thrives in ordinary soils, including limy ones. About 4 ft (1.2 m) high, it has whorled leaves and Turk's cap flowers of purplish red spotted with dark purple, in June and July; there is a fine white variety. Also useful on limy soils is *L. henryi*, 5–8 ft (1.5–2.5 m) in height, whose arching stems carry apricot-yellow flowers in August. These tend to fade if grown in full sun, as do the orange-yellow blooms of *L. hansonii*, which is 3–5 ft (90 cm–1.5 m) tall. In the same height range, the tiger lily, *L. lancifolium* (*L. tigrinum*), produces bright orange-red, heavily spotted, recurved flowers in August and September; the variety *splendens* is later flowering. The 4–7 ft (1.2–2 m) tall panther lily, *L. pardalinum*, succeeds in very moist soil, having orange-red flowers spotted with purple in July. The unusual Caucasian lily, *L. szovitsianum*, is suitable for both limy and peaty soils. The somewhat bell-shaped flowers, canary-yellow with black spots and brown anthers, appear in June (see p.41).

Liriope

Worth a place in the shade, although of thinner growth there and less floriferous, *L. muscari* makes clumps of broad grassy leaves. The violet-blue flowers, on stiff spikes about 1 ft (30 cm) high, open in August and resemble grape hyacinths. It is equally good as groundcover or for edging a path.

Maianthemum

The neatly carpeting *M. bifolium* is so named because of the paired leaves, like small lily-of-the-valley leaves. Heads of tiny white flowers appear in May. It makes a thin drift, appreciating cool peaty soil.

Oxalis

A dainty woodland carpeter, 'Rosea' is a soft pink form of the wood sorrel, *O. acetosella*. Flowering in spring, it is about 4 in. (10 cm) high and has pale green, clover-like leaves. It increases rapidly from self-sown seed (see p.6).

Podophyllum

The May apple, *P. peltatum*, is an unusual plant for a moist shady site. Some 1 ft (30 cm) tall, the large lobed leaves push up through the ground in spring, followed by white flowers in June and often by red fruits. The slightly taller *P. hexandrum (P. emodi)* has blush-pink cup-shaped blooms and large, shiny red fruits. Both spread slowly from the fleshy roots (see p.52).

Polygonum

Although many of the knotweeds are too invasive to consider for the garden, *P. affine* is an excellent ground-covering plant for cool moist soil. The narrow, deep green leaves turn vivid bronze-red in winter and spikes of rosy red flowers appear in autumn. The cultivar 'Darjeeling Red' has richer-coloured flowers.

Primula

A large number of primulas enjoy dappled shade and lend themselves to a woodland atmosphere, mingling well with other plants like lilies and trillium. However, they must have permanently moist, deep soil and many do best in wet conditions, by the banks of a stream or even in a bog (see p.56).

The common primrose, *P. vulgaris*, is a delightful edging plant for woodland, where the soil is moist and heavy, and increases itself freely. The beautiful sub-species *sibthorpii*, with masses of lilac-pink flowers in March, is easily propagated by division after flowering. Also suitable for such a position is *P. juliae*, a mat-like creeping plant with wine-red purplish flowers in April. It is usually represented in cultivation by stronger-growing hybrids, such as 'Wanda', with claret-coloured blooms, and the soft pink 'Garryarde Guinevere' (see p.53).

Left: the curious *Podophyllum hexandrum* is a natural woodlander

Right: the flowers of *Pulmonaria angustifolia* are pink in bud, opening to blue

The popular polyanthus comes in a wide range of colours, including blue, yellow, red, pink and white. It is usually raised from seed and flowers over many weeks in spring.

Pulmonaria

Active shade-lovers and valuable for their clump-forming habit, the lungworts are easily grown in any cool moist soil. The old spotted dog or soldiers and sailors, *P. officinalis*, grows to some 1 ft (30 cm) and has heart-shaped white-spotted leaves, usually lasting through the winter, and pretty nodding flowers, which open pink and then turn blue, in spring. Very similar but often considered superior are *P. saccharata* and its forms. The smaller *P. angustifolia*, with long, narrow, dark green leaves and sprays of pure blue flowers, thrives even in dense shade. The earliest to flower, starting in February, is the evergreen *P. rubra*, with coral-red bells.

Tellima

Forming attractive clumps of bright green, rounded or heart-shaped leaves, *T. grandiflora* carries small creamy bells on 2 ft (60 cm) stems from April to June. It is easily grown in the cool shadow of trees or tall shrubs and is happy in town gardens.

Left: 'Wanda', a very free-flowering hybrid of *Primula juliae*

Right: *Trillium grandiflorum* is the commonest of the wood lilies

Tiarella

The foam flower, *T. cordifolia*, is an excellent, low, carpeting plant for cool leafy soil, with rich green, maple-like foliage, bronze-tinted in autumn, and numerous feathery spikes of creamy white flowers in May and June. The taller *T. wherryi*, about 9 in. (22 cm), has light green ivy-shaped leaves and is less spreading in growth.

Trillium

The wake robin, *T. grandiflorum*, is very effective when planted in woodland or among shrubs, provided the soil is moist. It grows 1–1½ ft (30–45 cm) high and has stalkless leaves in threes and three-petalled flowers, white becoming flushed with pink in April and May.

Vancouveria

Similar to *Epimedium* (p.49), *V. hexandra* is a useful ground-covering plant some 1 ft (30 cm) high, with small, nodding, umbrella-shaped, white flowers in spring, above elegant, divided, soft green leaves. It is ideal for town gardens and accepts dry soil.

SHADE UNDER TREES

Patches of shade cast by individual trees are a frequent problem. Depending on the density of shade, however, it should be possible to grow the majority of plants recommended for permanent shade (pp.13–22) in these difficult dry conditions. One exception is *Choisya ternata*, which does not appreciate overhanging branches. It is also worth experimenting with some of the plants mentioned under dappled shade (pp.41–53), for example, *Gaultheria shallon*, *Tellima*, *Cyclamen* and *Primula*. Further suggestions are made below.

Bulbs and other spring-flowering plants offer another solution, since they come into growth early in the season before the tree canopy has formed. Wild snowdrops, are ideal for naturalizing under trees, together with winter aconites (see p.47) and early crocuses like *C. tommasinianus*, followed by bluebells.

Shrubs

Juniperus

The vigorous *J. × media* 'Pfitzeriana' will grow even under a cedar tree and is also excellent on a steep slope or bank. The spreading arching branches reach 6–8 ft (1.8–2.5 m) high and across and carry feathery, blue, juvenile leaves among the darker adult foliage. Like all junipers, it tolerates chalky soil.

Perennials

Anemone

As its name implies, the wood anemone, *A. nemorosa*, is well pleased with a situation among or directly beneath deciduous trees and will quickly multiply, especially on heavy soils. The native species bears dainty flowers, white flushed pink, on 6–8 in. (15–20 cm) stems in March and April. There are named forms like 'Robinsoniana', with lavender-blue blooms. Another small anemone, *A. apennina* usually flowers slightly later, in sky-blue. Forms with white or pink and with double flowers also occur. Even the beautiful Japanese anemone, *A. × hybrida* (see p.25), can make a contribution in early autumn.

Lamium

Yellow archangel, *L. galeobdolon* 'Variegatum', (*Galeobdolon luteum* 'Variegatum', *G. argentatum*) is one of the most effective

Anemone apennina makes a carpet of dainty leaves and flowers

groundcovers under trees or large shrubs. Some 1 ft (30 cm) high, it becomes a carpet of dark green and white-marbled foliage and produces yellow dead-nettle flowers in late spring. It is extremely vigorous and likely to smother smaller plants.

Luzula

The rampageous woodrush, *L. maxima* (*L. sylvatica*), is a grass 1–3 ft (30–90 cm) tall, with broad, green, tufted leaves and pale brown flowers. It should always be used with discretion, because of its greedy roots, but is invaluable for larger areas under trees and for steep banks and other awkward sites.

Polygonatum

Adaptable and easily grown, Solomon's seal, *P. multiflorum*, has long arching stems to 3 ft (90 cm), clad with attractive shiny leaves and, in May and June, hung with numerous whitish green bells. It and its commoner hybrid, *P.* × *hybridum*, delight in cool woodland, but will grow in almost any sort of shade.

Smilacina

The false spikenard, *S. racemosa*, is related to Solomon's seal and closely resembles it apart from the small open flowers, which are carried in a creamy white, scented spray at the end of the stem.

MOIST SHADE

Moisture and shade provide a perfect combination for many plants. A number of those already described prefer to be grown in soil which never dries out,including *Brunnera macrophylla*, *Cimicifuga racemosa*, *Gentiana asclepiadea*, *Podophyllum*, *Polygonum affine* and *Pulmonaria*. *Ajuga reptans* and *Aruncus dioicus* do best in damp, even boggy conditions.

Several ferns revel in a moist shady position, among them *Matteucia struthiopteris*, *Onoclea sensibilis* and *Osmunda regalis*. Eye-catching foliage plants for the waterside are *Rodgersia aesculifolia* and the smaller *R. pinnata* 'Superba'. The vast genus *Primula* contains many true moisture-lovers, such as *P. denticulata*, *P. florindae*, *P. alpicola* and *P. japonica* cultivars. (For details, see the Wisley handbook, *Water Gardens*.)

CLIMBERS FOR TRAINING INTO TREES

In the wild, many climbing shrubs use deciduous trees for support, with their roots and lower stems in shade and their flowering parts emerging through the branches into sunlight. This idea can easily be adapted for the garden and adds another dimension of interest, particularly where space is limited.

Once again, however, the help given by the tree in providing support is partially offset by competition from its roots. One way round this is to dig a large hole and place a bottomless wooden box in it, fill it with good soil and then plant the climber in it. The box will eventually rot, by which time the climber should be well established. This precaution is not necessary if the tree is old or if the climber has aerial roots, for example *Hydrangea* and *Schizophragma* (p.32 and p.35). The planting hole should be made at least 3–4 ft (90 cm–1.2 m) from the base of the trunk, which will also reduce competition from the roots. The climber can be trained into the tree along a bamboo cane, pole or wires, tying it loosely if required. Most climbers will do no harm to their hosts, but it would obviously be unwise to choose a very strong-growing plant like a vine for a small apple tree.

Many of these climbers also make excellent groundcover for difficult places, but must be kept within bounds and prevented from smothering other plants.

Above: the cultivars of *Primula japonica* are ideal for moist shade

Below: *Clematis montana* (left), a familiar sight in May and June with its profusion of blossom;
Lonicera japonica 'Halliana' (right), a rampant evergreen honeysuckle

Suitable climbers include *Actinidia chinensis, Akebia trifoliata, Clematis montana, Lonicera japonica* 'Halliana', *L. tragophylla, Rosa filipes* 'Kiftsgate' and *R. helenae* (see p.57). (For details, see the Wisley handbook, *Climbing and wall plants*).

ALPINES AND DWARF PLANTS FOR SHADE

Raised beds and sinks or troughs offer a convenient modern alternative to the rock garden, particularly where space is lacking, and the presence of shade need not be a deterrent. A number of dwarf plants tolerate or actually prefer shade, including *Campanula portenschlagiana, Chiastophyllum oppositifolium, Erinus alpinus* 'Mrs Boyle' and 'Dr Hanaele', *Hacquetia epipactis, Omphalodes cappadocica, Primula auricula* and *P. marginata* forms and *Ramonda myconi*. (For details, see the Wisley handbook, *Alpines the easy way*).

Some plants can also be grown in crevices on the shady side of a stone or brick retaining wall – round a terrace or raised bed perhaps. Ferns like *Asplenium ruta-muraria, A. trichomanes, Ceterach officinarum* and *Polypodium vulgare* are particularly useful.

Sharply drained soil is a prerequisite for alpines. However, in a shaded sink, raised bed or wall, where the rain rarely penetrates, conditions tend to be excessively dry. They can be improved by incorporating organic matter, which helps to retain moisture.

Spring-flowering dwarf bulbs are also good in a raised bed or trough, although they may look less attractive when they have finished flowering and the leaves are dying down (see p.60 for suggestions). For further recommendations, see *Anemone, Athyrium, Blechnum, Cyclamen, Tiarella, Viola*.

Left; the pink-flowered *Erinus alpinus* is excellent for a shady wall

Right: *Hacquetia epipactis*, a valuable shade-loving alpine

Left: the superb *Omphalodes cappadocica* flourishes in partial shade

Right: shade is essential to the lovely *Ramonda myconi*

CONTAINERS IN SHADE

Shade in the garden often goes hand in hand with poor or dry soil, as well as a shortage of space, and here containers have distinct advantages, since the essential elements – growing medium, drainage, watering – are all under control. A loam-based compost, such as John Innes No. 3, is best for shrubs and trees in large containers, while one of the proprietary peat-based composts would suit smaller plants. Both types normally contain an adequate supply of fertilizer. Free drainage can be ensured by making holes in the base of the container (if they are not already there) and then putting a layer of broken flower pots, pieces of brick or stones in the bottom, before filling up with compost. Watering is a matter of judgement and, although containers will dry out less quickly in the shade than in sun, they may not receive much rain from above.

Because the most important factors are taken care of, containers allow a wider range of plants to be grown in shade than might otherwise be possible. A permanent feature can be made of shrubs and perennials, while bulbs, bedding plants and annuals can be used at will. The short-term plants are particularly valuable for achieving quick results and contributing a splash of colour where it is most wanted. (See also the Wisley handbook, *Gardening in ornamental containers*.)

Plants recommended for containers in shade are as follows:

Shrubs

Aucuba japonica (p.14)
Buxus sempervirens (p.14)
Camellia japonica (pp.22–3)
C. × williamsii (pp.22–3)
Choisya ternata (p.14)
Clematis (p.30)
Euonymus fortunei var. *radicans* (p.31)
× *Fatshedera lizei* (pp.14–15)
Fatsia (p.16)
Hedera helix (p.16)
Ilex aquifolium (p.16)
Prunus laurocerasus (p.17)
P. lusitanica (p.24)
Rhododendron (pp.43–5)
Rosa (pp.33–5)
Taxus baccata (pp.18–19)
Vinca major (p.19)
V. minor (p.19)

Perennials

Bergenia (p.27)
Hosta (pp.27–8)
Lilium (especially *L. auratum*) (p.50)

Annuals (pp.39–41)

Asperula orientalis
Begonia semperflorens
Impatiens (busy lizzie)
Lobelia erinus
Nicotiana (tobacco plant)
Primula (polyanthus)
Viola (pansy)

Spring-flowering bulbs are excellent and easy plants for containers in shade, always welcome for their early display. Dwarf kinds are best, especially in a window box or round the base of a shrub in a large container. The choice could include crocuses, chionodoxas, scillas and grape hyacinths; daffodils, for instance, *Narcissus cyclamineus* and its cultivars; irises such as *Iris reticulata*; and tulip species like *Tulipa fosteriana* and *T. greigii* and their hybrids.

Bulbs which are slow to establish, notably snowdrops, winter aconites, snowflakes (*Leucojum vernum*) and *Anemone blanda* are better given a permanent home in a raised bed or trough (see p.58).

Finally, a mention for one of the finest of all container plants, the fuchsia. These beautiful tender shrubs flower almost as well in shade as in sun, continuing for several months in summer and autumn. Among the numerous cultivars are neat bushy forms for pots and window boxes, cascading types for hanging baskets and others for training into standards or pyramids. There is a wide range of colours, from pure white through pinks and reds to vivid violet, and some have variegated or golden foliage. Fuchsias can be kept going from year to year, so long as they are stored in a

Left: *Lilium auratum*, a beautiful lily for growing in a pot

Right: common box, *Buxus sempervirens*, is a decorative feature in an urn

frost-free place in winter, and they are also easily propagated from cuttings. (See also the Wisley handbook, *Fuchsias*.)

GROUNDCOVER IN SHADE

Groundcover has a particular application to planting in shade and it may have been noticed that the majority of plants already described carpet the ground in one way or another.

Groundcover is valuable for dealing with problem situations – steep slopes and banks, bare patches under trees and other places where grass will not grow or mowing is difficult. On a bank the plants can help to stabilize the earth and prevent erosion. It is best to use vigorous shrubs which root along the stems, like periwinkle, not herbaceous perennials. (See also the Wisley handbook, *Ground cover plants*.)

Grass itself is said to be the best groundcover and is certainly the most tolerant of being walked on, but it rarely succeeds in shade. Even the special grass seed mixtures available for the purpose are often unsatisfactory and stand only a little mowing. In a small shady area, therefore, ground-covering plants offer a practical and more rewarding alternative to grass. A larger expanse of lawn in shade could be replaced by paving and dotted with plants in containers (see p.59). Dwarf rock plants and ferns might be inserted between the gaps in the paving and many of those already recommended (p.58) would be effective.

Index of plants

Numbers in bold refer to illustrations

Opposite: *Viola labradorica*, an invasive but pretty violet for a shady spot